Little People, BIG DREAMS
JESSE OWENS

Written by
Maria Isabel Sánchez Vegara

Illustrated by
Anna Katharina Jansen

To: Zeb + Boone
From: Uncle Cheston's
Wild Family "out WEST"!

2022

Frances Lincoln
Children's Books

Little Jesse was the youngest child of the Owenses, a humble family of farmers from Alabama. He was the tenth and last of his siblings, but when his mother called for dinner, he beat everyone else to the table.

At school, no one could catch him! His gym teacher was
so impressed that he asked him to join the track team
after school. But Jesse had to run to work repairing
shoes and delivering groceries to support his family.

Of course, that didn't stop Jesse. He decided to practice in the morning, when the sun was rising and everyone was still in bed. He was determined to become the best athlete in the world.

Jesse's first lesson was to imagine that the track was on fire. Even though that wasn't true, it helped him develop his own elegant running style, keeping his feet off the ground as much as possible.

He entered Ohio State University, where everybody called him
the "Buckeye Bullet." Jesse became the first African American
captain of a university team and the first who had to work
as a lift operator in order to pay for his schooling.

Despite Jesse's success on the track, he had to wait for his teammates to take their showers before he could wash himself. All around him, life was separated for black people and white people.

100 YARDS
9,4 sec

LONG JUMP
8,13 m

During one single championship, Jesse set three world records and tied a fourth…in only 45 minutes! It was one of the most celebrated moments in the history of sports, and a good chance for Jesse to prove himself before the Olympic Games.

220 YARDS

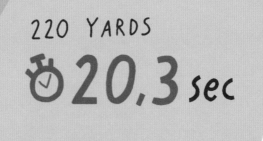 20,3 sec

220 YARDS
LOW HURDLES

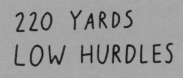 22,6 sec

The Olympics were held in Berlin, Germany. In 1936, the country was ruled by a terrible man named Adolf Hitler. Hitler believed that white athletes were superior because they were white. Jesse won a gold medal and stole the spotlight from Hitler's hateful regime.

More than 110,000 people stayed to watch Jesse win three more gold medals over the next few days.
He was an Olympic hero, the fastest man in history, but still a humble person, happy to hug his toughest rival.

When Jesse arrived home, there was a dinner in
his honor. But—as soon as he got there—
he realized nothing had changed. He could not even
use the main doors to reach his own reception.

Sadly, soon after, no one remembered Jesse's amazing achievements and he had to take any job to make a living. He worked at a gas station, toured with a jazz band, and even accepted a race against horses.

He had retired when he finally got his most valuable award:
the Presidential Medal of Freedom, the highest honor
for any American. No athlete embodied the struggle
against injustice and racism more than Jesse.

And every time the Olympic Games take place, little Jesse is remembered. The humble boy who fought the wind and sought out new sights, running just on the strength of his feet and the courage of his lungs.

JESSE OWENS

(Born 1913 • Died 1980)

1930

1932

Born the son of a farmer and a grandson of slaves, Jesse Owens was the youngest of ten children. Jesse and his siblings grew up helping their father harvest cotton on the land he farmed, working long hours in the fields of Lawrence County, Alabama. Here, Jesse ran barefoot, finding time to play in breaks between work. When he was nine, his family left the South in search of a better life, settling in Cleveland, Ohio. There, Jesse worked in a shoe repair shop after school to bring in extra income for his family, which meant that he couldn't train with the school's athletics team. Luckily, his junior high track coach recognized his potential, and allowed him to practice in the early morning hours before school began. Jesse caught national attention during his school years in both sprints and long jump, but made headlines in college in

1936   1976

1935 when he set three world records and tied a fourth, all in the space of about 45 minutes. Nicknamed the "Buckeye Bullet," Jesse went on to represent his country at the 1936 Olympic Games in Germany, where Adolf Hitler criticized America for allowing black athletes to compete. At the games, Jesse won four gold medals, infuriating Hitler and challenging audiences around the world to stand up to racism. But back in America, Jesse faced the same prejudice when President Roosevelt failed to welcome him to the White House following his momentous win. This didn't deter Jesse: "Find the good," he said. "It's all around you. Find it, showcase it, and you'll start believing in it." Not just one of the world's most successful athletes, Jesse's attitude made him one of the most important role models for us today.

Want to find out more about **Jesse Owens?**

Read one of these great books:

Who Was Jesse Owens? by James Buckley Jr. and Gregory Copeland

Jesse Owens: Fastest Man Alive by Carole Boston Weatherford and Eric Velasquez

Brimming with creative inspiration, how-to projects, and useful information to enrich your everyday life, Quarto Knows is a favorite destination for those pursuing their interests and passions. Visit our site and dig deeper with our books into your area of interest: Quarto Creates, Quarto Cooks, Quarto Homes, Quarto Lives, Quarto Drives, Quarto Explores, Quarto Gifts, or Quarto Kids.

Concept and text © 2020 Maria Isabel Sánchez Vegara. Illustrations © 2020 Anna Katharina Jansen

First Published in the US in 2020 by Frances Lincoln Children's Books, an imprint of The Quarto Group. 400 First Avenue North, Suite 400, Minneapolis, MN 55401, USA.

www.QuartoKnows.com

First Published in Spain in 2020 under the title Pequeño & Grande Jesse Owens by Alba Editorial, s.l.u., Baixada de Sant Miquel, 1, 08002 Barcelona

www.albaeditorial.es

A catalog record for this book is available from the British Library.

ISBN 978-0-7112-4583-9

Set in Futura BT.

Published by Katie Cotton • Designed by Karissa Santos
Edited by Rachel Williams and Katy Flint • Production by Caragh McAleenan and Laura Grandi

Manufactured in Guangdong, China CC032020

9 7 5 3 1 2 4 6 8

Photographic acknowledgments (pages 28–29, from left to right) 1. Great American Sprinter Jesse Owens Married Ruth Soloman in Cleveland, 1930 © Keystone-France/Gamma-Keystone via Getty Images 2. Cleveland high school student and future Olympic champion Jesse Owens crossing a finish line to break the world 100-meter record, 1932 © New York Times Co via Getty Images 3. Jesse Owens at the start of the 200 meters at the 1936 Berlin Olympics, which he won in 20.7 seconds, an Olympic record, 1936 © Hulton Archive via Getty Images 4. U.S. Athlete Jesse Owens, photographed before leaving for Melbourne, 1976 © Antonin Cermak / Fairfax Media via Getty Images.

Collect the
Little People, **BIG DREAMS** series:

FRIDA KAHLO

ISBN: 978-1-84780-783-0

COCO CHANEL

ISBN: 978-1-84780-784-7

MAYA ANGELOU

ISBN: 978-1-84780-889-9

AMELIA EARHART

ISBN: 978-1-84780-888-2

AGATHA CHRISTIE

ISBN: 978-1-84780-960-5

MARIE CURIE

ISBN: 978-1-84780-962-9

ROSA PARKS

ISBN: 978-1-78603-018-4

AUDREY HEPBURN

ISBN: 978-1-78603-053-5

EMMELINE PANKHURST

ISBN: 978-1-78603-020-7

ELLA FITZGERALD

ISBN: 978-1-78603-087-0

ADA LOVELACE

ISBN: 978-1-78603-076-4

JANE AUSTEN

ISBN: 978-1-78603-120-4

GEORGIA O'KEEFFE

ISBN: 978-1-78603-122-8

HARRIET TUBMAN

ISBN: 978-1-78603-227-0

ANNE FRANK

ISBN: 978-1-78603-229-4

MOTHER TERESA

ISBN: 978-1-78603-230-0

JOSEPHINE BAKER

ISBN: 978-1-78603-228-7

L. M. MONTGOMERY

ISBN: 978-1-78603-233-1

JANE GOODALL

ISBN: 978-1-78603-231-7

SIMONE DE BEAUVOIR

ISBN: 978-1-78603-232-4

MUHAMMAD ALI

ISBN: 978-1-78603-331-4

STEPHEN HAWKING

ISBN: 978-1-78603-333-8

MARIA MONTESSORI

ISBN: 978-1-78603-755-8

VIVIENNE WESTWOOD

ISBN: 978-1-78603-757-2

MAHATMA GANDHI

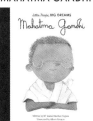

ISBN: 978-1-78603-787-9

DAVID BOWIE

ISBN: 978-1-78603-332-1

WILMA RUDOLPH

ISBN: 978-1-78603-751-0

DOLLY PARTON

ISBN: 978-1-78603-760-2

BRUCE LEE

ISBN: 978-1-78603-789-3

RUDOLF NUREYEV

ISBN: 978-1-78603-791-

ZAHA HADID

ISBN: 978-1-78603-745-9

MARY SHELLEY

ISBN: 978-0-7112-4639-3

MARTIN LUTHER KING JR.

ISBN: 978-0-7112-4567-9

DAVID ATTENBOROUGH

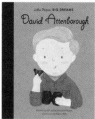

ISBN: 978-0-7112-4564-8

ASTRID LINDGREN

ISBN: 978-0-7112-5217-2

EVONNE GOOLAGONG

ISBN: 978-0-7112-4586-

BOB DYLAN

ISBN: 978-0-7112-4675-1

ALAN TURING

ISBN: 978-0-7112-4678-2

BILLIE JEAN KING

ISBN: 978-0-7112-4693-5

GRETA THUNBERG

ISBN: 978-0-7112-5645-3

JESSE OWENS

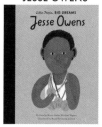

ISBN: 978-0-7112-4583-9

JEAN-MICHEL BASQUIAT

ISBN: 978-0-7112-4580-8

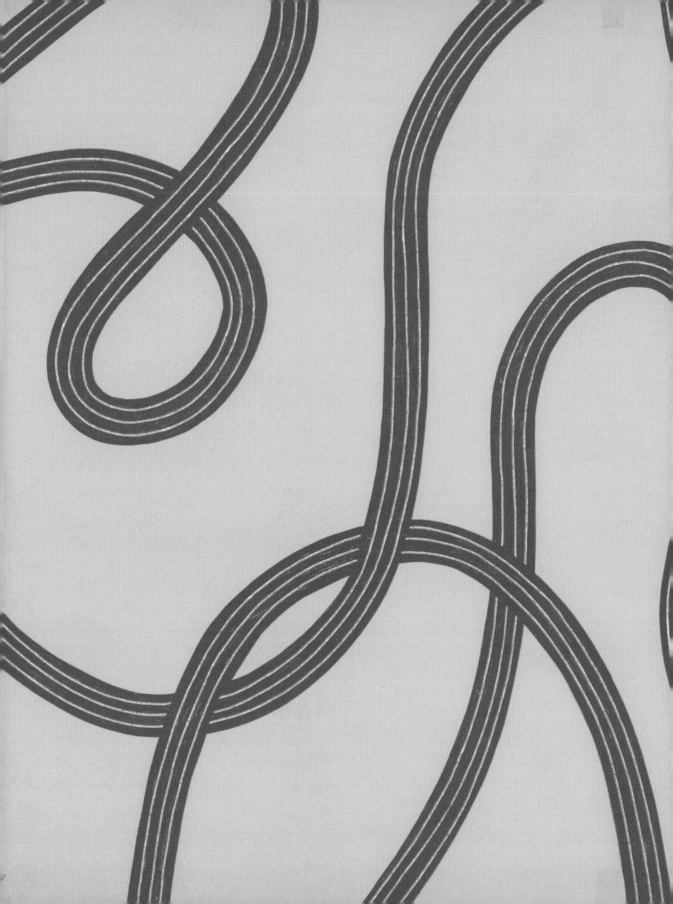